Cambridge Young Learners
English Tests

Cambridge Starters 4

Examination papers from

University of Cambridge
ESOL Examinations:

English for Speakers of Other Languages

CAMBRIDGE
UNIVERSITY PRESS

CAMBRIDGE UNIVERSITY PRESS
Cambridge, New York, Melbourne, Madrid, Cape Town, Singapore, São Paulo

Cambridge University Press
The Edinburgh Building, Cambridge CB2 2RU, UK

www.cambridge.org
Information on this title: www.cambridge.org/9780521611299

First published 2005
4th printing 2006

Printed in the United Kingdom at the University Press, Cambridge

A catalogue record for this publication is available from the British Library

ISBN-13 978-0-521-61129-9 Student's Book
ISBN-10 0-521-61129-6 Student's Book

ISBN-13 978-0-521-61130-5 Answer booklet
ISBN-10 0-521-61130-X Answer booklet

ISBN-13 978-0-521-61131-2 Cassette
ISBN-10 0-521-61131-8 Cassette

ISBN-13 978-0-521-61132-9 Audio CD
ISBN-10 0-521-61132-6 Audio CD

Contents

Test 1

Listening   5

Reading and Writing   11

Test 2

Listening   19

Reading and Writing   25

Test 3

Listening   33

Reading and Writing   39

Speaking Tests

Test 1   47

Test 2   51

Test 3   55

Part 1
– 5 questions –

Listen and draw lines. There is one example.

Part 2

– 5 questions –

Listen and write a name or a number.

There are two examples.

.... Nick

.... 8

1

....

2

....

3

....

4

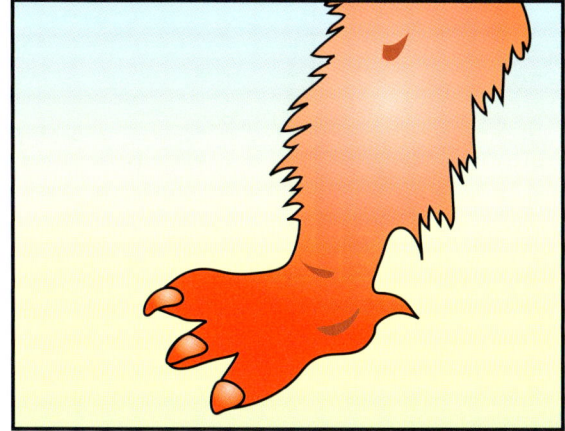

....

5

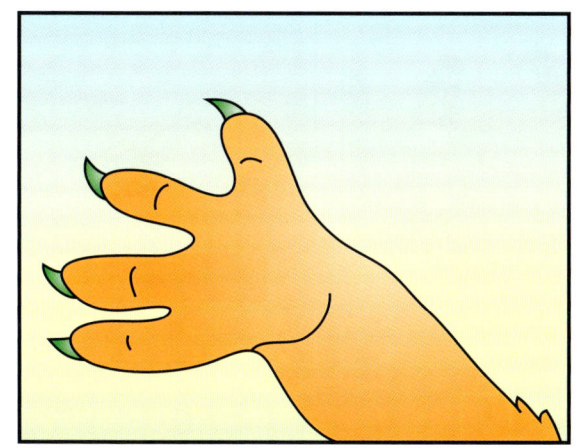

....

Part 3

– 5 questions –

Listen and tick (✔) the box. There is one example.

Which T-shirt can Sue wear today?

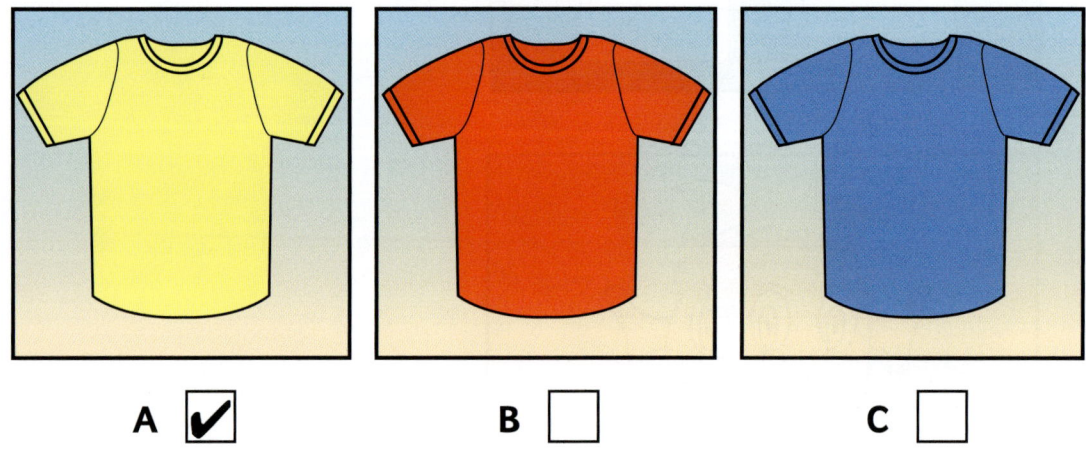

A ✔   B ☐   C ☐

1   What's Sam drawing?

A ☐   B ☐   C ☐

2   Which sport's on TV today?

A ☐   B ☐   C ☐

3   What's Grandfather doing?

A ☐   B ☐   C ☐

4   What does May want for breakfast?

A ☐   B ☐   C ☐

5   What's Kim doing?

A ☐   B ☐   C ☐

Part 4

– 5 questions –

Listen and colour. There is one example.

Reading and Writing

Part 1
– 5 questions –

**Look and read. Put a tick (✔) or a cross (✗) in the box.
There are two examples.**

Examples

This is a lemon.

This is an elephant.

Questions

1

This is a shoe.

2

This is an armchair.

3

This is a bathroom.

4

This is a lamp.

5

This is a fish.

Part 2

– 5 questions –

Look and read. Write yes or no.

Examples

The girl is riding a bike.

yes

There are some flowers in the tree.

no

Questions

1   Two rabbits are eating ice-cream.

2   The crocodile is sleeping under the tree.

3   The woman has got a green hat.

4   There are five monkeys in the water.

5   The boys are playing with toy boats.

Part 3
– 5 questions –

Look at the pictures. Look at the letters. Write the words.

Example

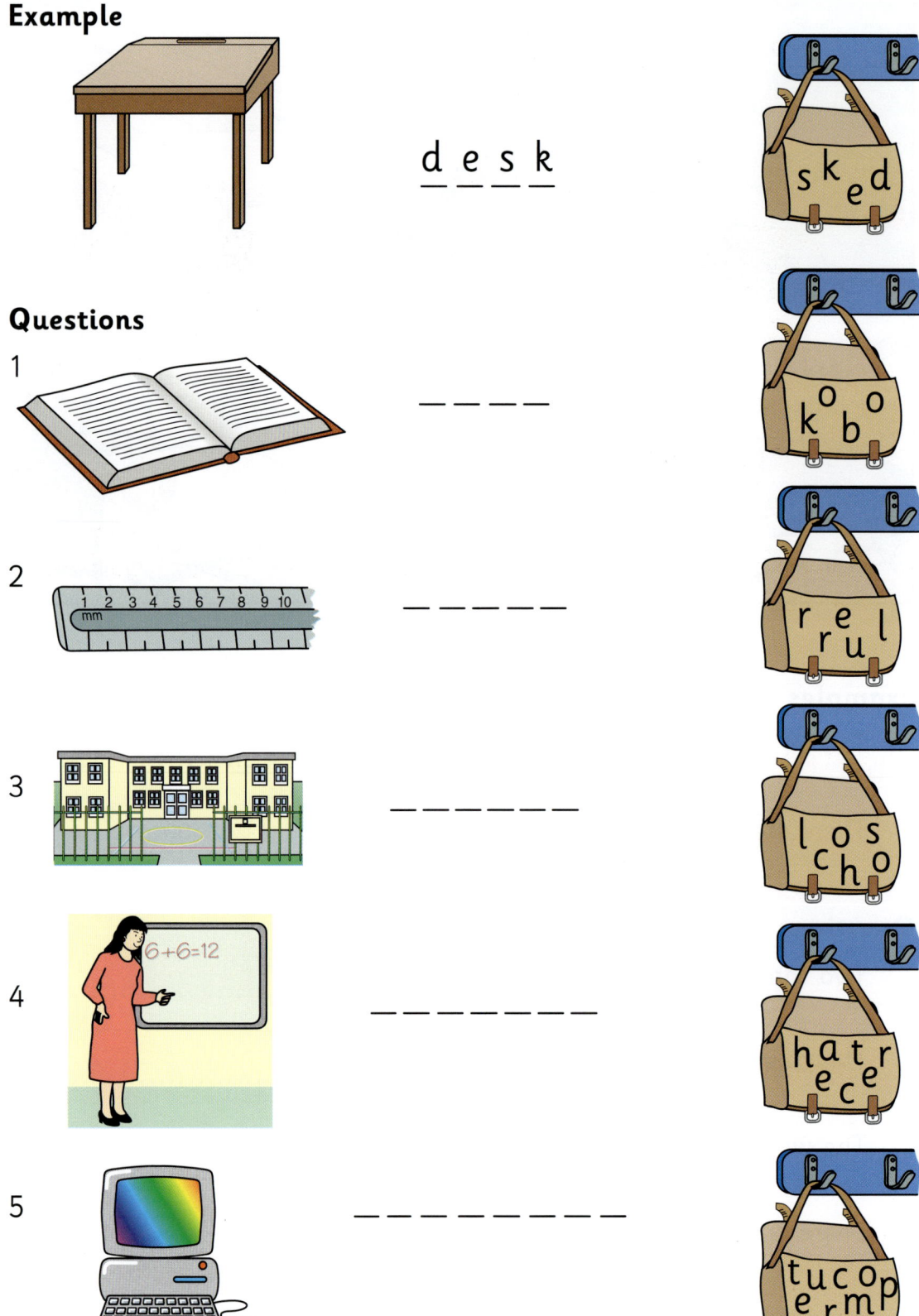

d e s k
_ _ _ _

Questions

1 _ _ _ _

2 _ _ _ _ _

3 _ _ _ _ _ _

4 _ _ _ _ _ _ _

5 _ _ _ _ _ _ _ _

Part 4
– 5 questions –

**Read the story. Look at the pictures and the two examples.
Write one-word answers.**

What am I?

I am a beautiful animal. I live next to a family with a big

.... house .... and a garden with .... flowers .... in it.

I have a long .... and ears. There is brown hair on

my body. I can run and jump with my four ....

I like .... I give them a ride. They give me a

....

What am I?

I am a __ __ __ __ __ .

Part 5
– 5 questions –

Look at the pictures and read the questions. Write one-word answers.

Examples

What is he eating?   an ....egg.............

How many apples are there?   ....three..............

Questions

1 What drink has he got?   some ....

2   What colour is the apple?   ....

3   Where is he going?   to   ....

4   Who is he giving the apple to?   a   ....

5   Where are they sitting?   on the   ....

Blank Page

Part 1
– 5 questions –

Listen and draw lines. There is one example.

Part 2
– 5 questions –

Listen and write a name or a number.

There are two examples.

...........................6...........................

...................Happy...................

1

....

2

....

3

....

4

....

5

....

Part 3

– 5 questions –

Listen and tick (✔) the box. There is one example.

What has Ann got in her bag?

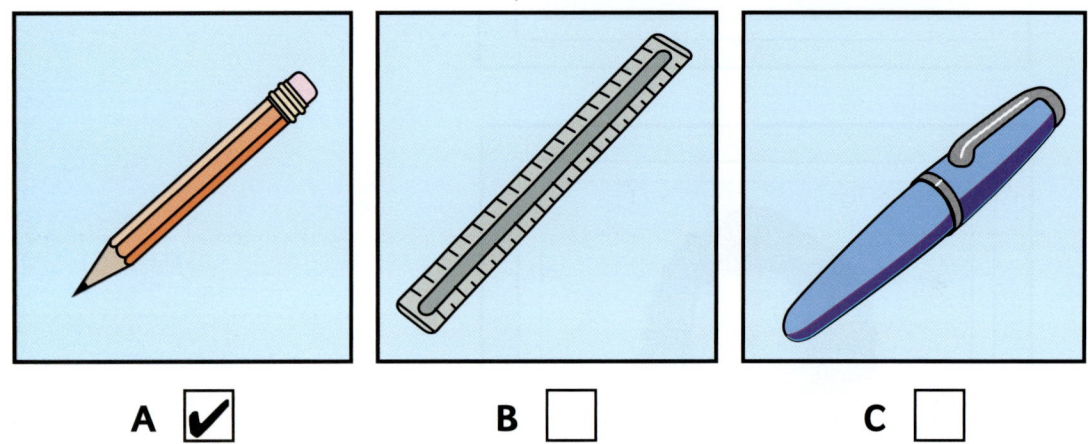

A ✔   B ☐   C ☐

1   Which is Nick's favourite sport?

A ☐   B ☐   C ☐

2   What is May buying?

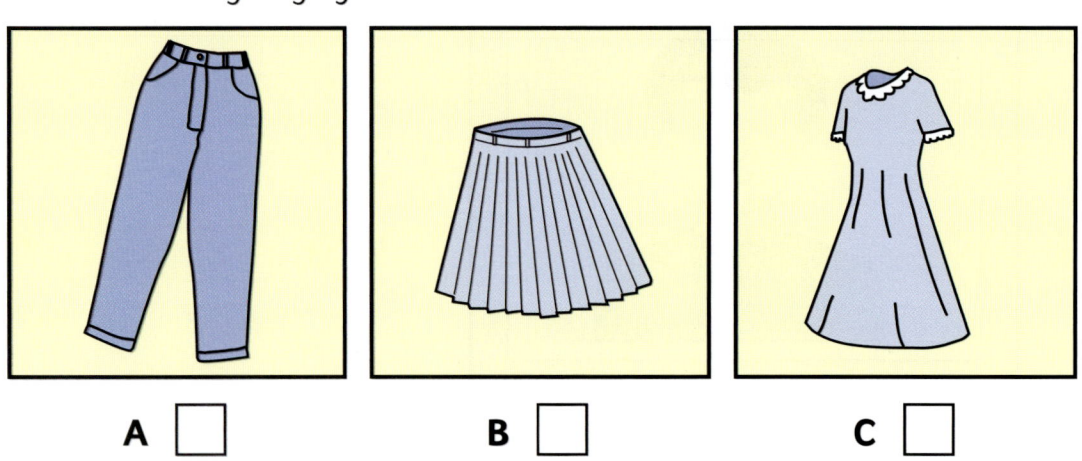

A ☐   B ☐   C ☐

3   Where's the camera?

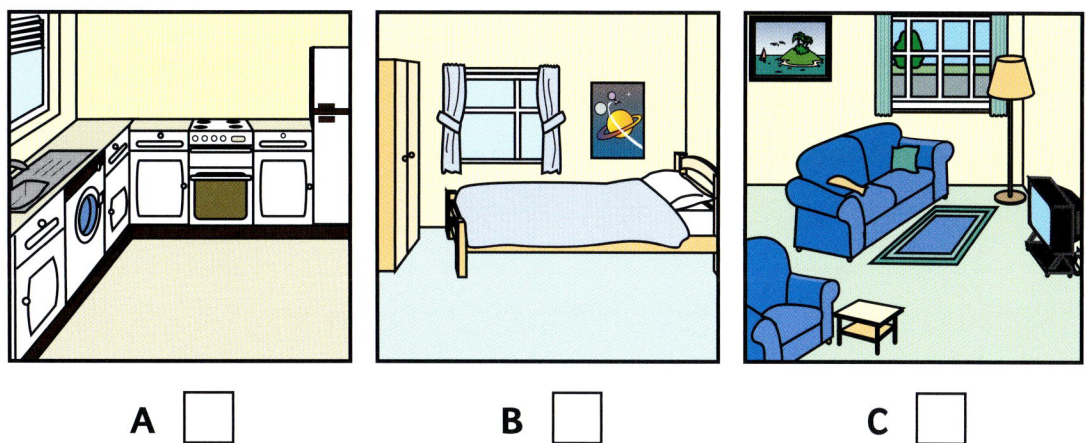

A ☐   B ☐   C ☐

4   Which man is Bill's teacher?

A ☐   B ☐   C ☐

5   What does Sam want for lunch?

A ☐   B ☐   C ☐

Part 4

– 5 questions –

Listen and colour. There is one example.

Reading and Writing

Part 1
– 5 questions –

**Look and read. Put a tick (✔) or a cross (✗) in the box.
There are two examples.**

Examples

This is a sheep.

This is a woman.

Questions
1

This is a pineapple. ☐

2

This is a sock. ☐

3

This is a potato. ☐

4

This is a box. ☐

5

This is a mouse. ☐

Part 2
– 5 questions –

Look and read. Write yes or no.

Examples

Two children are sitting on chairs.　　　*yes*
....

There are five boys in the room.　　　*no*
....

Questions

1　Four of the children are wearing hats.
....

2　There's a birthday cake on the table.
....

3　A boy has got a bird in his hand.
....

4　One of the girls is wearing a long dress.
....

5　A girl is bouncing a ball.
....

Part 3
– 5 questions –

Look at the pictures. Look at the letters. Write the words.

Example

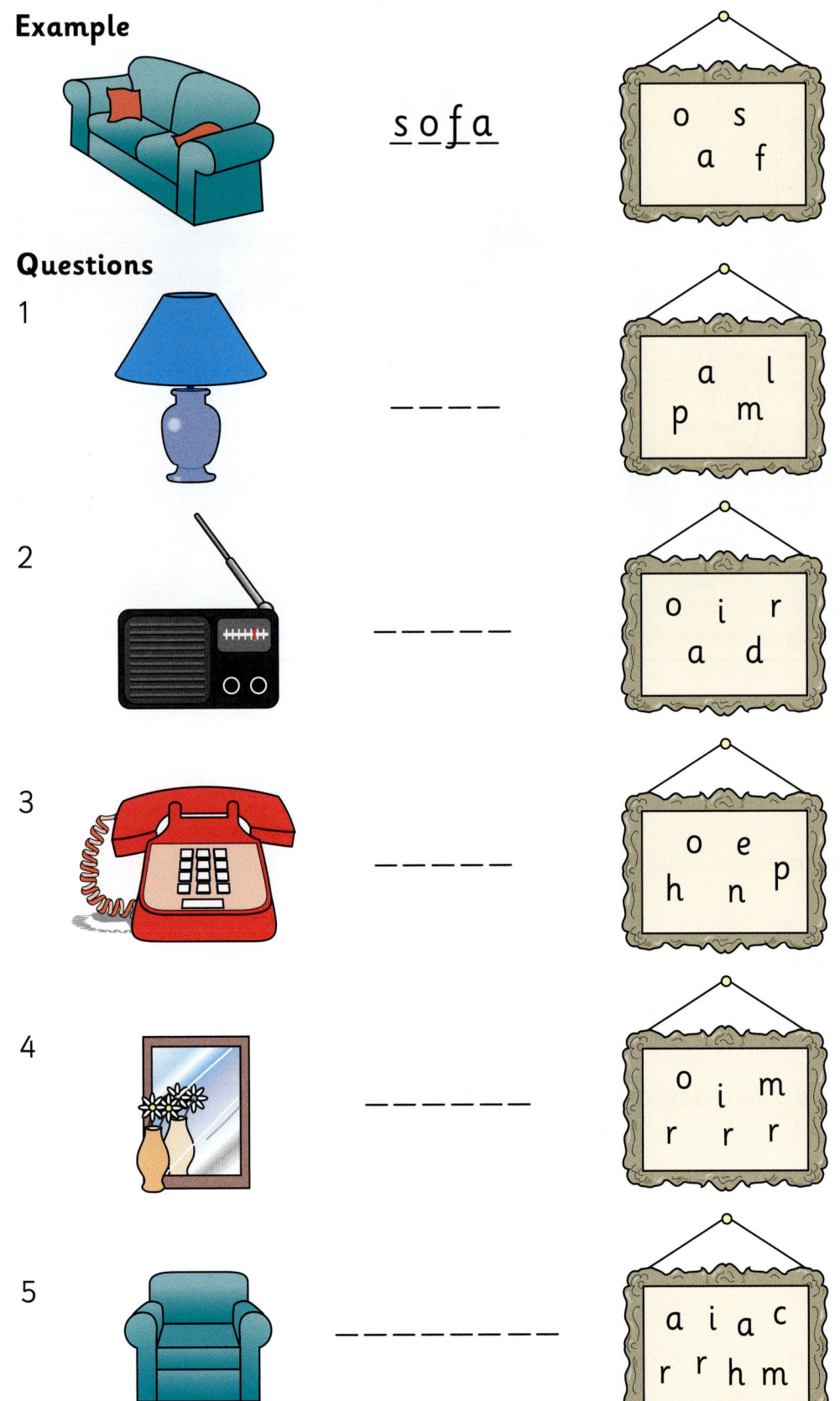

s o f a

Questions

1 _ _ _ _

2 _ _ _ _ _

3 _ _ _ _ _

4 _ _ _ _ _ _

5 _ _ _ _ _ _ _

Part 4

– 5 questions –

Read the story. Look at the pictures and the two examples.
Write one-word answers.

What am I?

I have ......windows...... , walls and a ......door...... . On my walls,

there are some paintings and a .... Children sit at

tables in me. They read and write in their .... or they

look at the .... I have a bookcase and two cupboards.

In one of them there are pens, ... and paint.

What am I?

I am a __ __ __ __ __ __ __ __ .

Part 5
– 5 questions –

Look at the pictures and read the questions. Write one-word answers.

Examples

Where is the man sitting?   on the   .... mat .....

What game are the two
boys playing?   .... football ....

Questions

1   What's the man playing?   a ....

2   Where's the ball?   in the ....

3   What are the ducks doing?   ....

4   How many people are playing
    football now?   ....

5   What has the dog got in its mouth?   the ....

Blank Page

Part 1
– 5 questions –

Listen and draw lines. There is one example.

Part 2
– 5 questions –

Listen and write a name or a number.

There are two examples.

.... Bill

.... 9

1

....

2

....

3

....

4

....

5

....

Part 3
– 5 questions –

Listen and tick (✔) the box. There is one example.

Which is Kim's lunch?

A ✔   B ☐   C ☐

1   Where's Ben's watch?

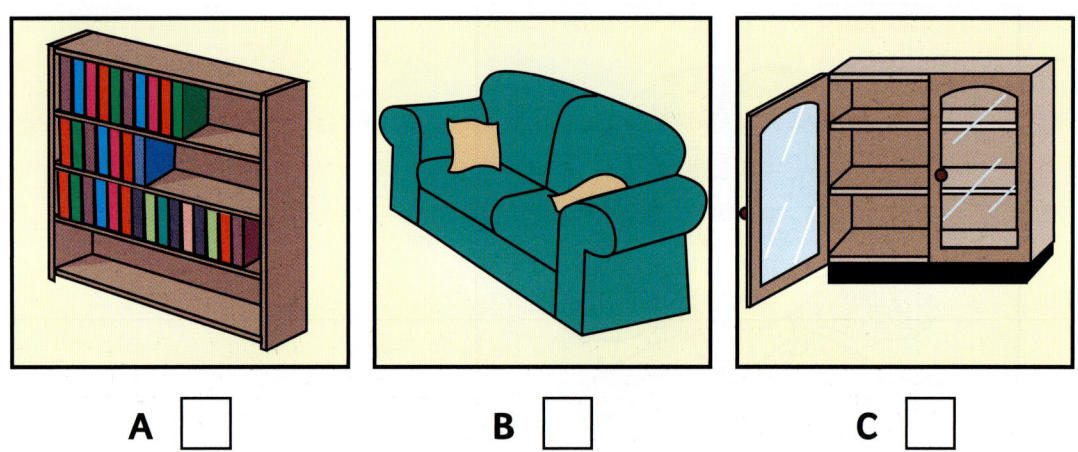

A ☐   B ☐   C ☐

2   What's the baby doing?

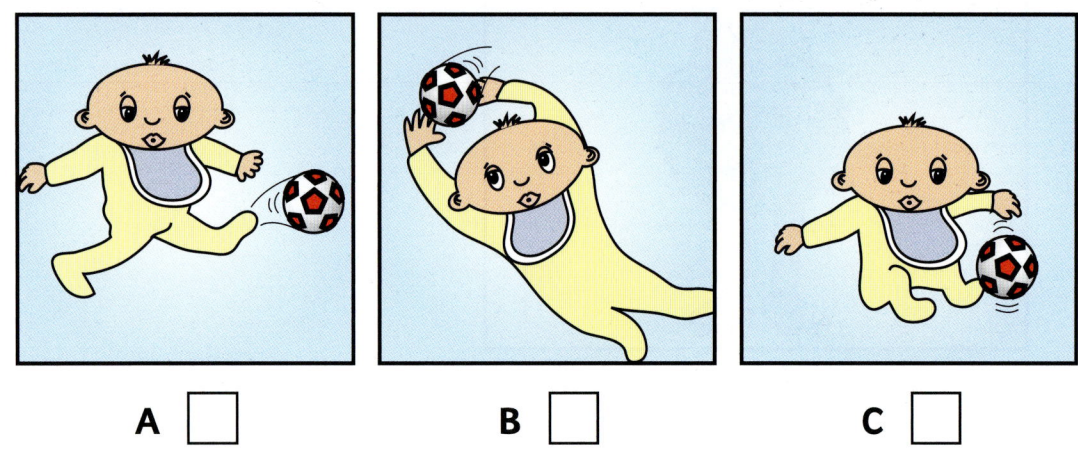

A ☐   B ☐   C ☐

3   Which is Sue's grandmother?

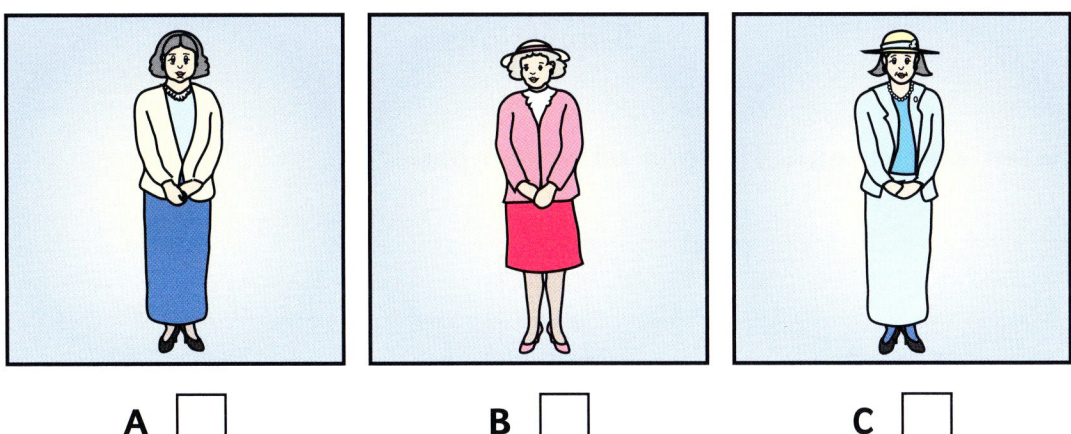

A ☐   B ☐   C ☐

4   Which is Ann's favourite drawing?

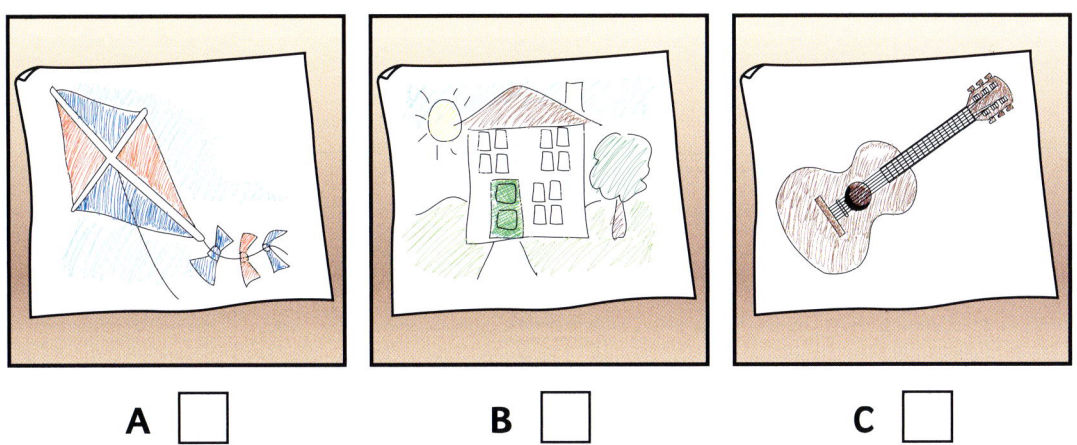

A ☐   B ☐   C ☐

5   What's Tom doing?

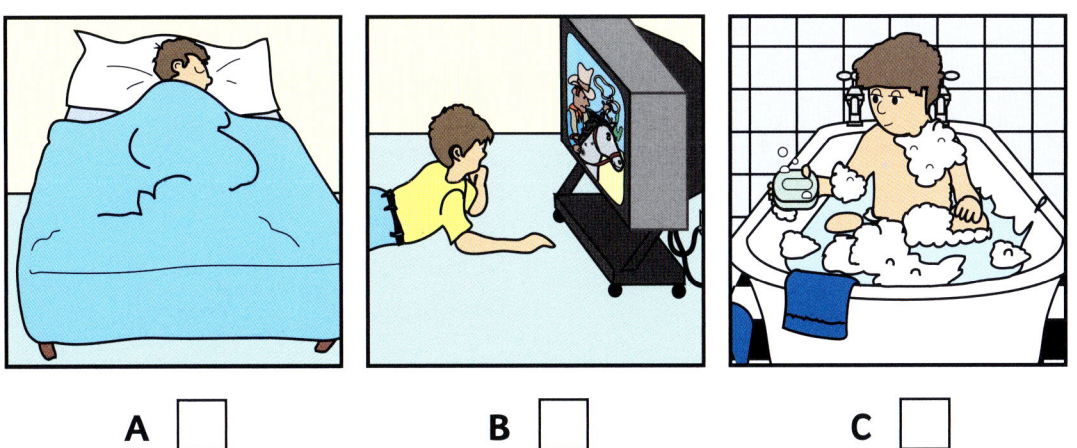

A ☐   B ☐   C ☐

Part 4

– 5 questions –

Listen and colour. There is one example.

Reading and Writing

Part 1
– 5 questions –

Look and read. Put a tick (✔) or a cross (✗) in the box.
There are two examples.

Examples

This is a frog.

This is a sofa.

Questions

1

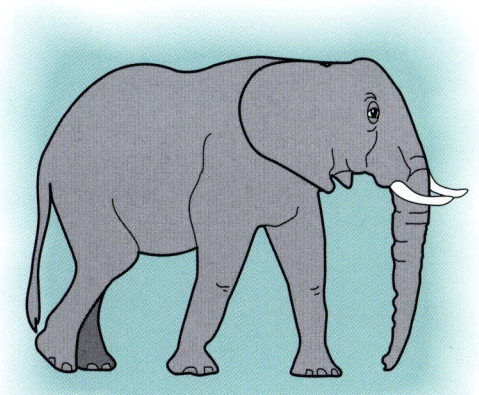

This is a crocodile.

2

This is a phone.

3

This is a jacket.

4

This is a pineapple.

5

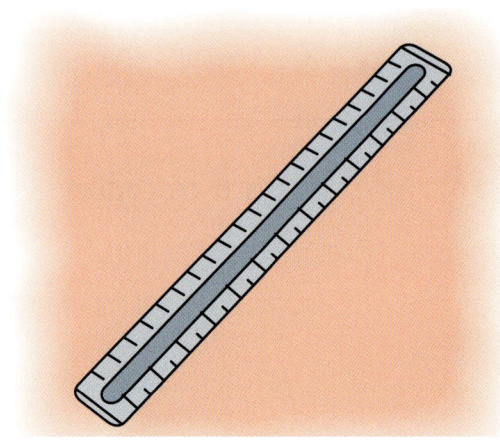

This is a ruler.

Part 2

– 5 questions –

Look and read. Write yes or no.

Examples

There are two women in the picture.   *yes*
....

This is a bookshop.   *no*
....

Questions

1   The dog is playing with a ball.
....

2   The baby is drinking some milk.
....

3   There are four apples on the floor.
....

4   The boy is picking up a hat.
....

5   The man has got a black bag.
....

Part 3

– 5 questions –

Look at the pictures. Look at the letters. Write the words.

Example

<u>f a c e</u>

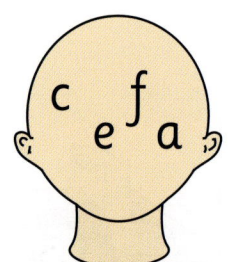

Questions

1

_ _ _ _

2   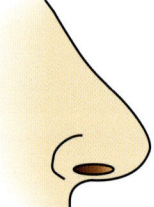

_ _ _ _

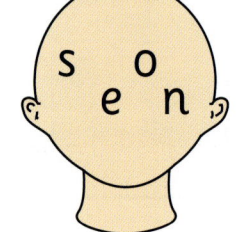

3   

_ _ _ _

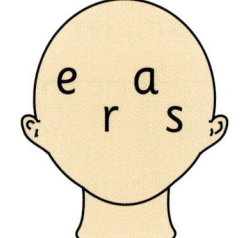

4   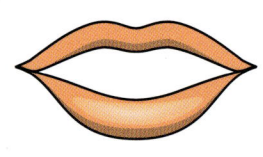

_ _ _ _

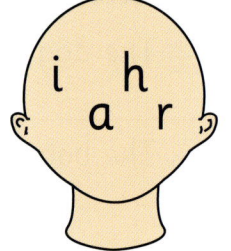

5   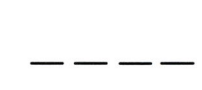

_ _ _ _ _

Part 4

– 5 questions –

**Read the story. Look at the pictures and the two examples.
Write one-word answers.**

What am I?

I stand in the ......classroom...... in front of the children and I say, 'Sit

on your ......chairs...... ' or, 'Look at the ....

please.' I give the children .... and they draw pictures.

Some children play on the .... In the afternoon their

mothers and fathers come and I open the .... and say,

'Goodbye.'

What am I?

I am a __ __ __ __ __ __ __ .

Part 5
– 5 questions –

Look at the pictures and read the questions. Write one-word answers.

Examples

Where is the family?   in the   .... Kitchen ....

What is the girl watching?   .... TV ....

Questions

1   What has the boy got in his hands?   a   ....

2   How many girls are there in the living room? ....

3   What is the girl with brown hair playing?   a ....

4   Where is the boy now?   in a ....

5   What is he doing?   ....

Blank Page

SCENE CARD

Blank Page

OBJECT CARDS

Test 1

Test 1

Test 1

Test 1

Test 1

Test 1

Test 1

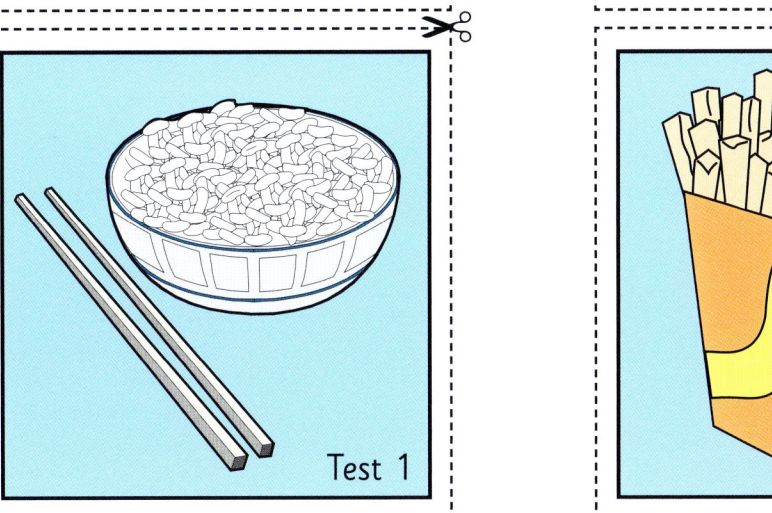

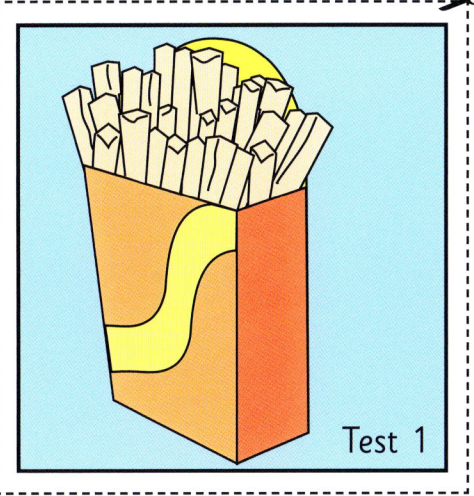

Test 1

Blank Page

Speaking

SCENE CARD

Blank Page

OBJECT CARDS

Test 2

Test 2

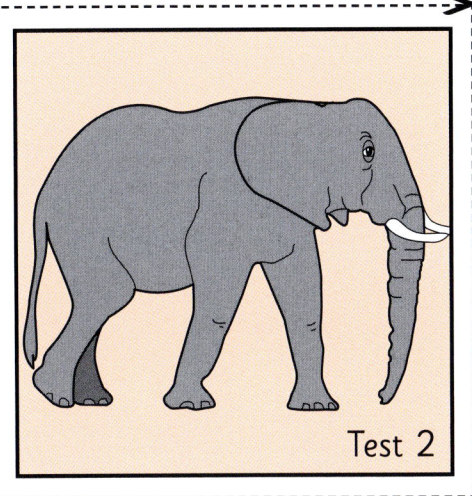

Test 2

Test 2

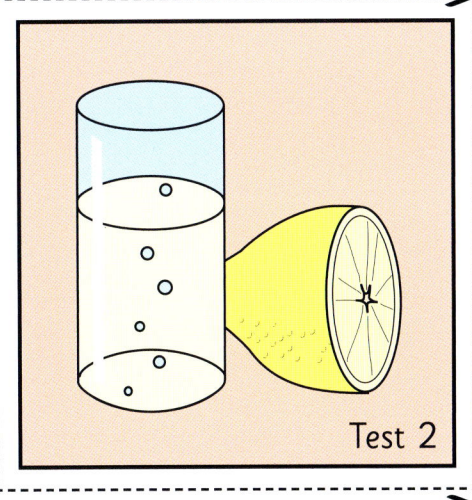

Test 2

Test 2

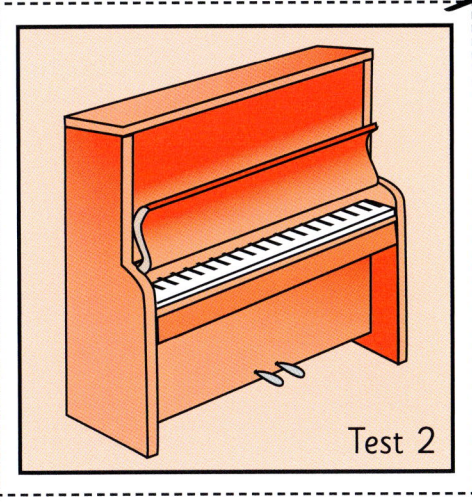

Test 2

Test 2

Blank Page

54

SCENE CARD

Blank Page

OBJECT CARDS

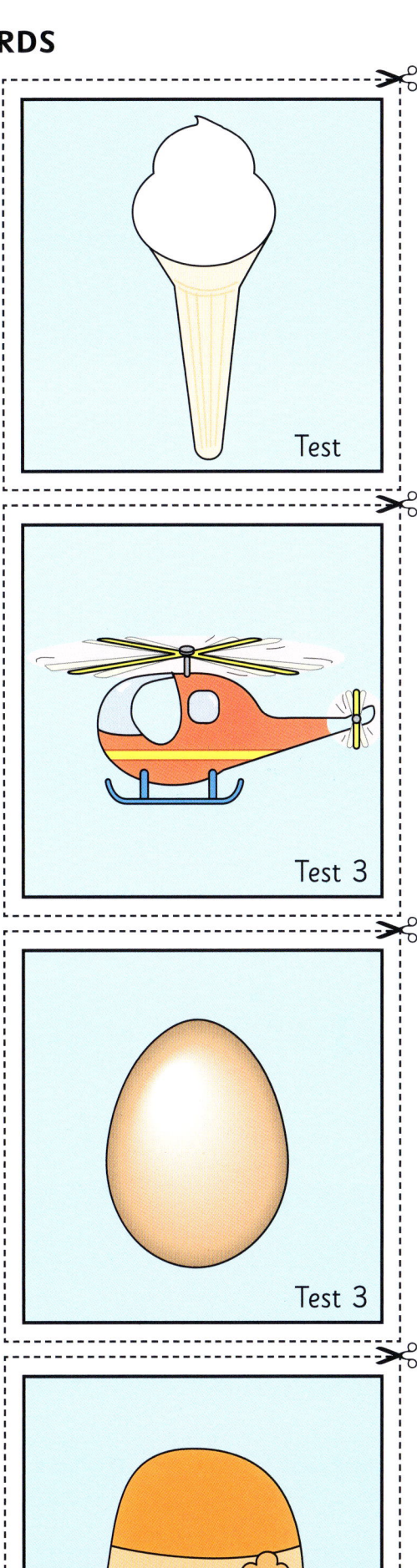

Test 3

Test

Test 3

Test 3

Test 3

Test 3

Test 3

Test 3

57